PIANO / VOCAL / GUITAR

CHART HITS
2022-2023
14 TOP SINGLES

ISBN 978-1-70518-858-3

Visit Hal Leonard Online at
www.halleonard.com

World headquarters, contact:
Hal Leonard
7777 West Bluemound Road
Milwaukee, WI 53213
Email: info@halleonard.com

In Europe, contact:
Hal Leonard Europe Limited
1 Red Place
London, W1K 6PL
Email: info@halleonardeurope.com

In Australia, contact:
Hal Leonard Australia Pty. Ltd.
4 Lentara Court
Cheltenham, Victoria, 3192 Australia
Email: info@halleonard.com.au

ANTI-HERO

Words and Music by TAYLOR SWIFT
and JACK ANTONOFF

Vocal sung an octave lower than written.

4

ing 'cause you got tired of my schem - ing. (For the last time.) It's
ing and life will lose all its mean - ing. (For the last time.)

me, hi, I'm the prob - lem, it's me. At tea - time,

ev - 'ry - bod - y a - grees. I'll stare di - rect - ly at the sun, _

___ but nev - er in ___ the mir - ror. It ___ must be ex-haust - ing al - ways

Vocal sung at pitch.

CELESTIAL

Words and Music by ED SHEERAN,
JOHNNY McDAID and STEVE MAC

Up-beat Pop

You see to-night,_ it could go ei-ther way,_ hearts bal-anced on a
I see the light_ shin-ing through the rain,_ a thou-sand col-ors in a

ra - zor blade._____ We are de-signed_ to love and break_ and to
bright - er shade._____ Need-ed to rise_ from the low-est place,_ there's_

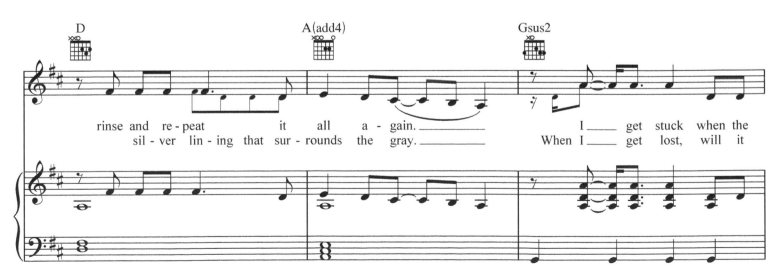

rinse and re-peat_ it all a-gain._____ I _ get stuck when the
sil-ver lin-ing that sur-rounds the gray._____ When I _ get lost, will it

LIFT ME UP
from BLACK PANTHER: WAKANDA FOREVER

Words and Music by ROBYN FENTY,
TEMILADE OPENIYI, LUDWIG GÖRANSSON
and RYAN COOGLER

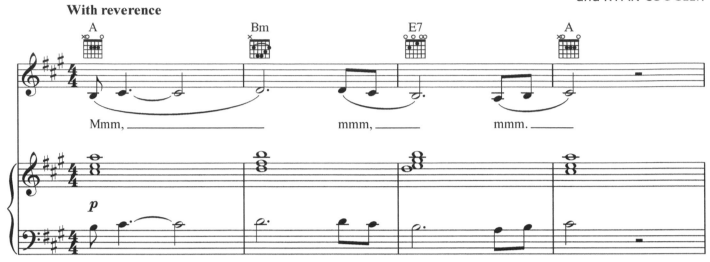

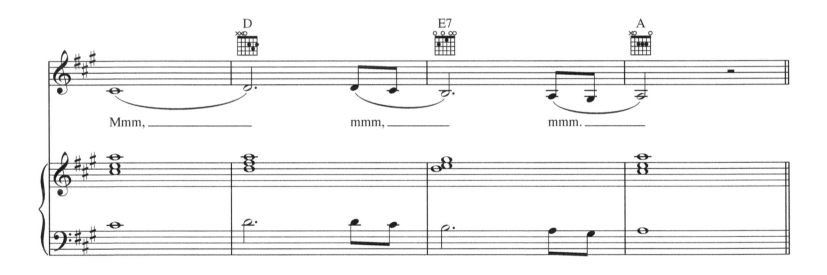

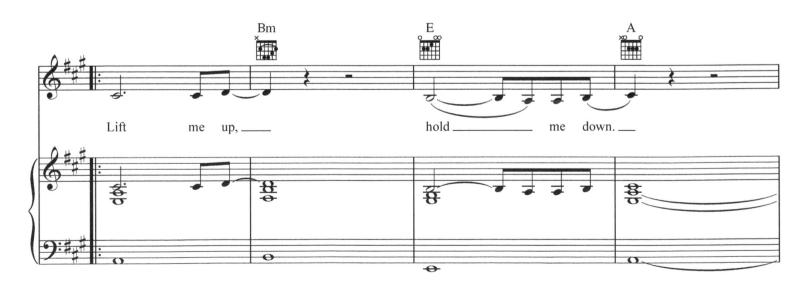

FLOWERS

Words and Music by MILEY RAY CYRUS,
MICHAEL POLLACK and GREGORY HEIN

Disco Pop

We were good, _____ we were gold. _____ Kind of dream _____
_____ cher - ry red, _____ match the ros -

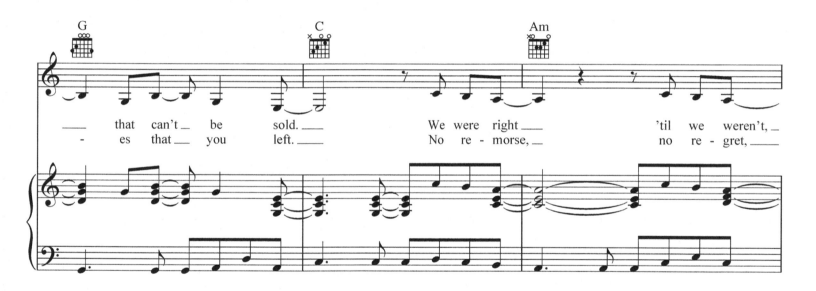

_____ that can't _ be sold. _____ We were right _____ 'til we weren't, _____
- es that _ you left. _____ No re - morse, _____ no re - gret, _____

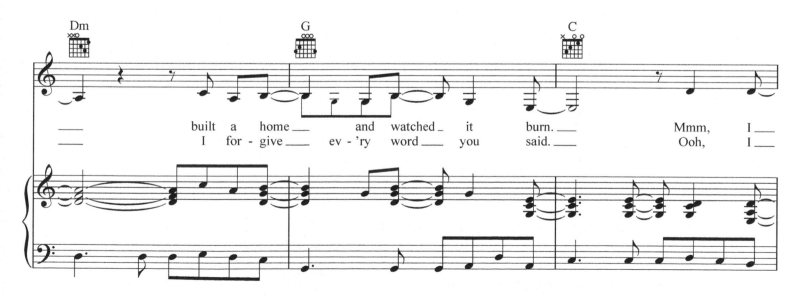

_____ built a home _____ and watched _ it burn. _____ Mmm, I _____
_____ I for - give _ ev - 'ry word _ you said. _____ Ooh, I _____

2

C   G/B   Am   Dm

can love me bet - ter, ba - by.   Can love me bet - ter,   I ____ can love me bet - ter, ba - by.

G   C

Can love me bet - ter,   I.
Oh,   I. _____   I ____

Am   Dm

____ did - n't want to leave ____ you,   I _____ did - n't want to fight. ____   Start -

E7   **D.S. al Coda**

- ed to cry, ____ but then re - mem - bered   I... ____

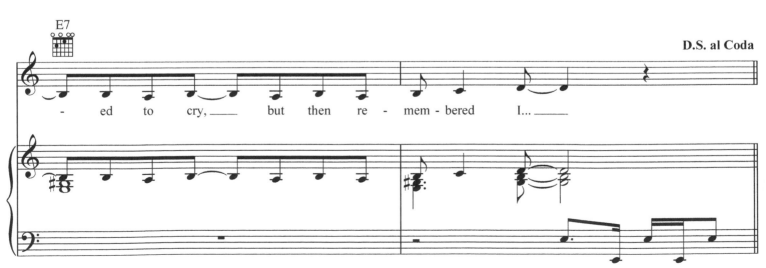

FORGET ME

Words and Music by LEWIS CAPALDI,
BEN KOHN, PETE KELLEHER,
PHILIP PLESTED, TOM BARNES
and MICHAEL POLLACK

Moderate Pop Rock

Days ache and nights are long, two years and still you're not

gone. Guess I'm still hold-ing on.

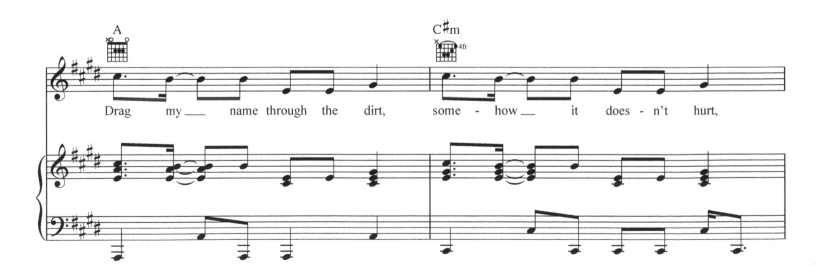

Drag my name through the dirt, some-how it does-n't hurt,

GOLDEN HOUR

Words and Music by JAKE LAWSON
and ZACHARY LAWSON

Moderately, in 1

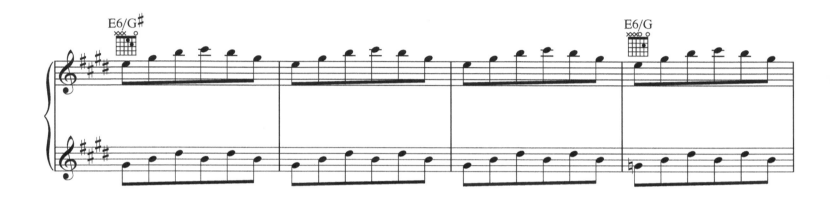

To Coda

Oh, _____ oh.

We were just two lov-ers, feet up on the dash, driv-ing no-where fast.

Burn-ing through the sum-mer, ra - di - o on blast, make the mo-ment last.

She got so - lar pow-er: min-utes feel like hours. _

40

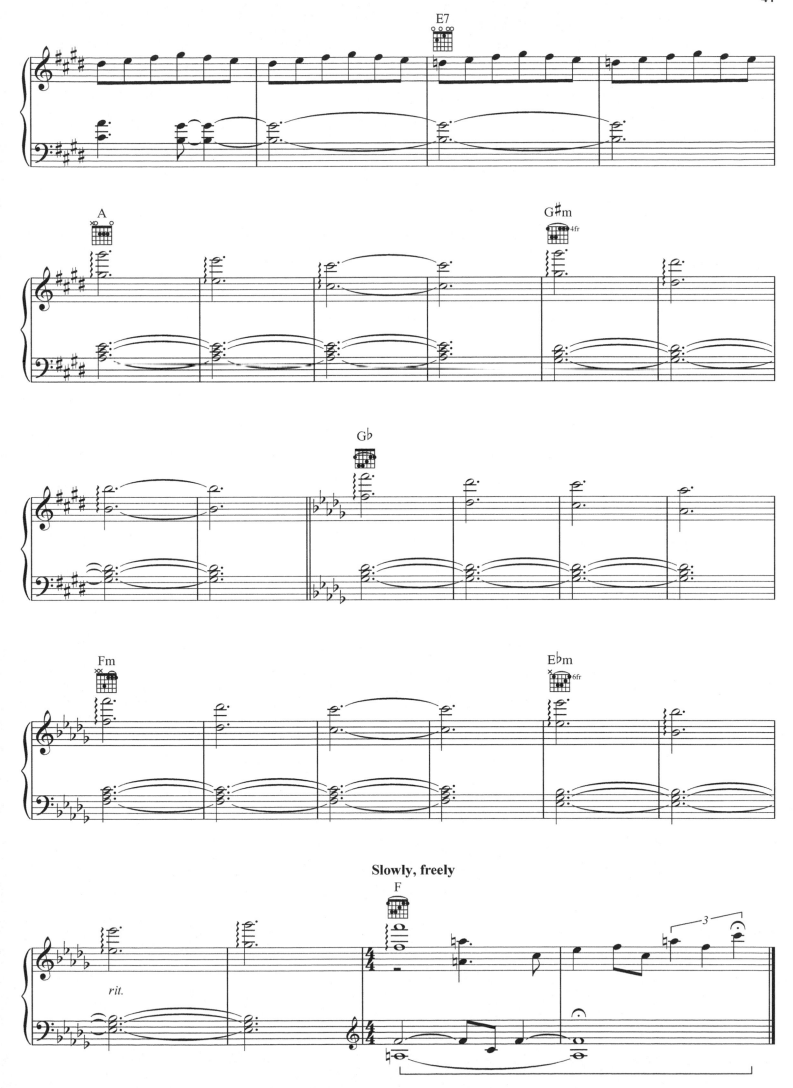

I AIN'T WORRIED

from TOP GUN: MAVERICK

Words and Music by RYAN TEDDER,
BRENT KUTZLE, TYLER SPRY,
BJÖRN YTTLING, JOHN ERIKSSON
and PETER MOREN

With a groove

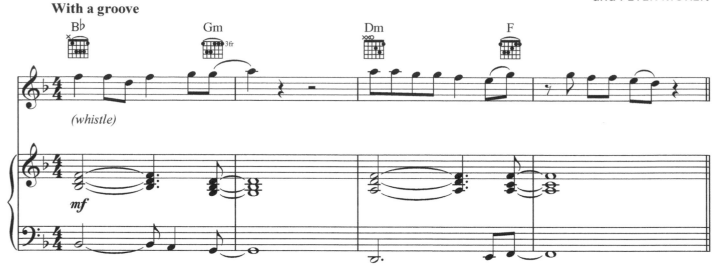

(whistle)

I don't know what you've been told, ___ but time is run-ning out, no need ___

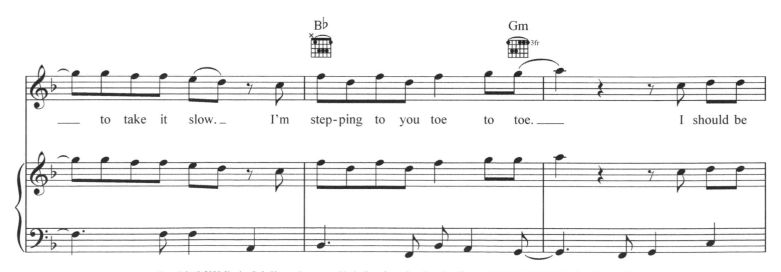

___ to take it slow. ___ I'm step-ping to you toe to toe. ___ I should be

QUIETLY YOURS
featured in the Netflix film PERSUASION

Words and Music by
JASMINE VAN DEN BOGAERDE

same as be - fore. Man - y years have gone by,

but I knew you'd come.

Qui - et - ly keep - ing this

hope in my heart. Prayed the night bring

SOMETHING IN THE ORANGE

Words and Music by
ZACHARY LANE BRYAN

Moderately fast, in 1

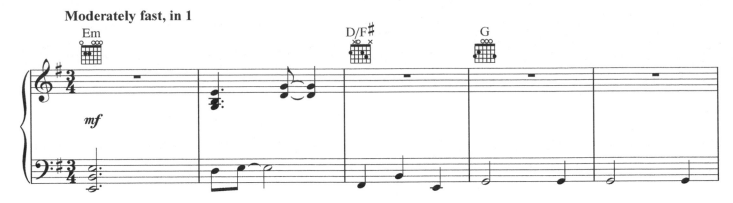

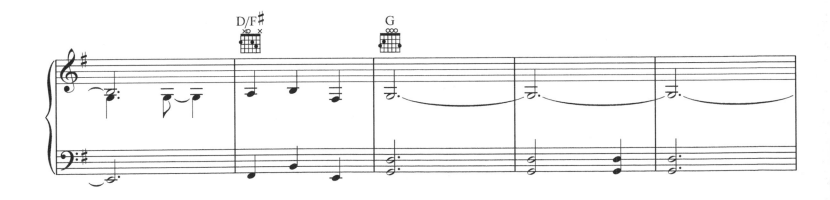

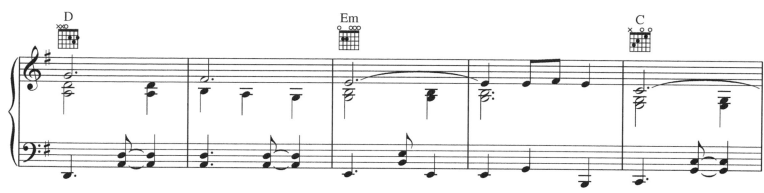

Need to hear you say you've been wait - ing all ___

wood used to creak.

home.

SUNROOF

Words and Music by NICHOLAS MINUTAGLIO,
NICHOLAS URE and AIDAN RODRIGUEZ

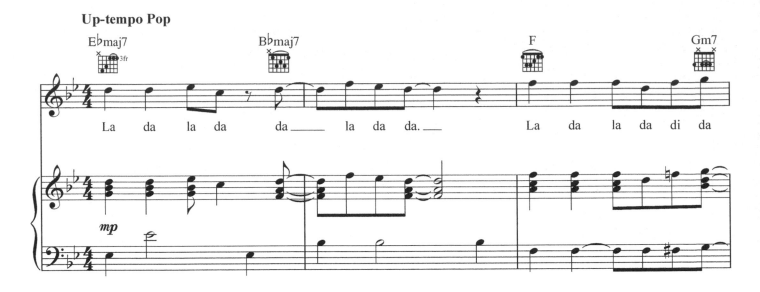

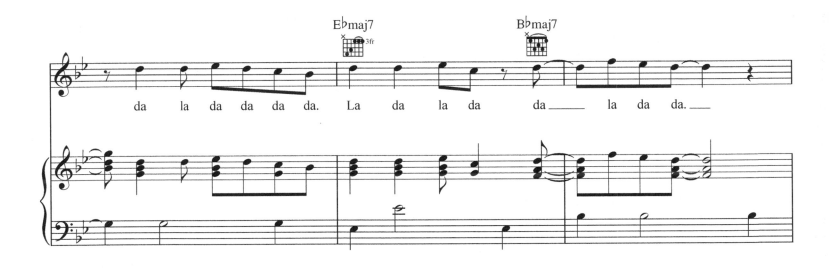

TV

Words and Music by BILLIE EILISH O'CONNELL
and FINNEAS O'CONNELL

UNHOLY

Words and Music by SAM SMITH,
ILYA SALMANZADEH, HENRY WALTER,
BLAKE SLATKIN, OMER FEDI,
JAMES NAPIER and KIM PETRAS

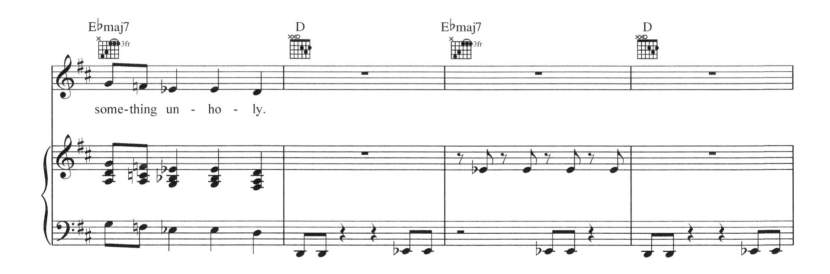

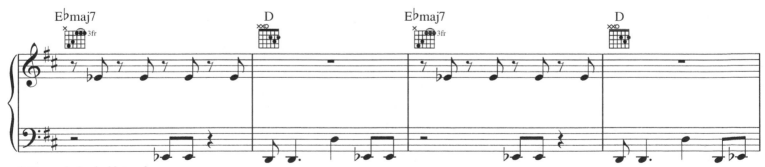

Recorded a half step lower.

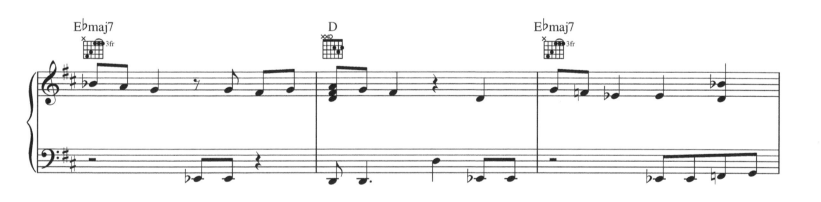

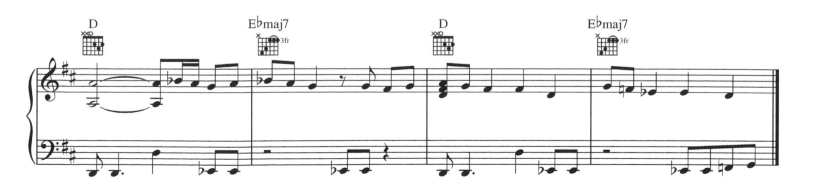

VICTORIA'S SECRET

Words and Music by DAN HENIG,
MARK NILAN JR. and JACQUELINE MISKANIC

God, I wish some-bod-y would have told me when I was young-er that all bod-ies aren't __ the same.

Pho-to-shop, it-ty bit-ty mod-els on mag-a-zine cov-ers told me I was o-ver-weight.

I stopped eat-ing, what a bum-mer. Can't have carbs and a hot girl sum-mer.

* Recorded a half step lower.

LOVE POWER
from DISENCHANTED

Music by ALAN MENKEN
Lyrics by STEPHEN SCHWARTZ